Date: 6/15/16

J 954 BAI
Bailer, Darice,
India /

INDIA

by Darice Bailer

Published by The Child's World®
1980 Lookout Drive • Mankato, MN 56003-1705
800-599-READ • www.childsworld.com

Acknowledgments
The Child's World®: Mary Berendes, Publishing Director
Red Line Editorial: Editorial direction
The Design Lab: Design
Amnet: Production

Design elements: Shutterstock Images; Srijan Roy Choudhury/
Shutterstock Images
Photographs ©: Shutterstock Images, cover (left top), cover (right),
cover (left bottom), 1 (top), 1 (bottom right), 9, 11, 14 (right), 22,
27, 30; Srijan Roy Choudhury/Shutterstock Images, cover (left
center), 1 (bottom left), 14 (left); Pius Lee/Shutterstock Images, 5;
Alexander Mazurkevich/Shutterstock Images, 6–7; Daniel Rao/
iStock/Thinkstock, 8; Daniel Berehulak/Getty Images News/
Thinkstock, 13; Byelikova Oksana/iStock/Thinkstock, 15;
Guido Cozzi/Atlantide Phototravel/Corbis, 16 (left); Frederic
Soltan/Corbis, 16 (right); Natalia Davidovich/Shutterstock
Images, 19; Jan S./Shutterstock Images, 21; Pete Niesen/
Shutterstock Images, 23; Tukaram Karve/Shutterstock Images, 24;
Kijja Pruchyathamkorn/Shutterstock Images, 25; Pablo Rogat/
Shutterstock Images, 26; Thinkstock, 28

ISBN 9781634070478
LCCN 2014959729

Printed in the United States of America
Mankato, MN
July, 2015
PA02268

ABOUT THE AUTHOR

Darice Bailer is the author of many books for children. She is delighted to write about India.

TABLE OF CONTENTS

ARCTIC
OCEAN

ATLANTIC
OCEAN

PACIFIC
OCEAN

PACIFIC
OCEAN

INDIA

INDIAN
OCEAN

SOUTHERN
OCEAN

SCALE

0   1000 Miles

0   1000 KM

N
W   E
S

INDIA

India's land is about one-third the size of the United States. More than 1 billion people live in India.

FUN FACT · ONE WORLD · MANY COUNTRIES

30ap

CHAPTER 1

WELCOME TO INDIA!

Roosters crow across India. The morning sun is a bright yellow ball. It hangs low over New Delhi, India's capital. Though it is early, the city's streets are already crowded and noisy. Motorcycles and bicycles dart around cars. Cars honk and dodge goats in the road. Children walk to school or ride there in rickshaws.

At school, many teachers greet their students in English. Hindi is the official language of India. But English is important

Indian children crowd onto a rickshaw to get a ride to school. Schools in India do not provide buses for students.

for doing business around the world. Parents want their kids to learn English. It will help them get jobs one day.

Not all children in India are able to attend school. Many families are so poor that the children must help earn money. Some children work on farms or in factories. Others sit outdoors in the market every day. They sell fruit, vegetables, or spices. The money they earn helps feed their families.

Whether they earn money or attend school, these children all call India their home. India is a large country in South Asia. It has more people than any other country, except China.

India is a land of color and culture. Women dress in bright, colorful saris. Many children live with their parents and grandparents at home.

India's population is growing quickly. This has created a large group of people who need jobs. Indians work for companies throughout the world. Their work is making India a successful country.

Indian markets are colorful, busy places. This woman is selling spices at a market in Goa, India.

THE LAND

India has many beaches. Thottada Beach is along the Arabian Sea.

India is the seventh largest country in the world. The country is a **peninsula**. It stretches from the Himalayan Mountains to the Indian Ocean. India has six neighbors. They are the countries of Pakistan, China, Nepal, Bhutan, Bangladesh, and Myanmar (Burma). India also has many islands in the Arabian Sea and Bay of Bengal.

Because India is a peninsula, it has miles of coastline. The Arabian Sea splashes on India's western shores. The Bay of Bengal ripples in the east. In between, the land is very different. There are snowy mountains and hot, sandy deserts. There are rain forests and plains.

The Himalayas separate India from the rest of Asia. They are the highest mountains in the world. The highest peak in India is Kanchenjunga. At 28,208 feet (8,598 m), it is the world's third tallest mountain.

The Indus, Ganges, and Brahmaputra rivers run down the mountains. The rivers pick up dirt. They carry it with them as they

During the monsoons, Kanchenjunga receives heavy snowfall.

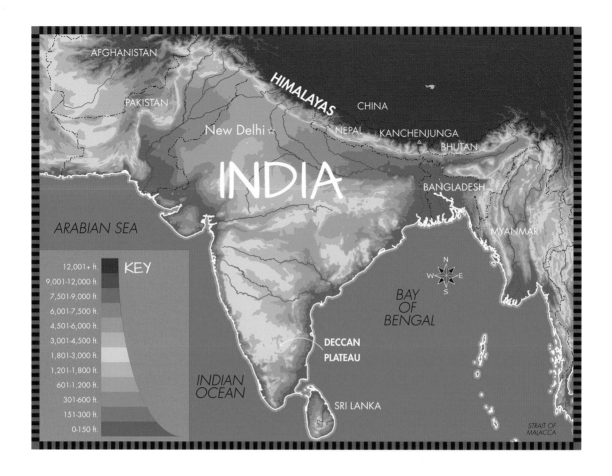

wind through the flat land below. The soil they spill in the northern plains makes excellent farmland. Rice, wheat, and other crops grow well here. This food feeds India and the rest of the world.

Most of the Deccan **Plateau** is also farmland. The plateau is in central and southern India. Part of this plateau is forest. It is home to elephants, monkeys, and other wildlife. Mother elephants nudge babies along with their trunks. Crocodiles rest on the banks of the Kabini River.

The Himalayan Mountains in the northeast block cold winds from Asia. India has a tropical climate. Summer is hot.

The temperature can reach 123 degrees Fahrenheit (50 degrees C) in the desert. After India's summer come the monsoons. Monsoons are strong winds that blow across the Indian Ocean toward land. Rain falls and helps the country cool off.

India's land is rich in natural resources. Diamonds are mined from the earth. These gems are one of India's biggest **exports**. Iron ore is a rock that is used to make steel. It is also found in India. The country is the world's largest producer of iron ore and coal.

The Bengal tiger is India's national animal. India is the only county in the world where both lions and tigers live in the wild.

FUN FACT

ONE WORLD · MANY COUNTRIES

CHAPTER 3

GOVERNMENT AND CITIES

India's official name is the Republic of India. It is the world's largest **democracy**. The United States holds a presidential election in one day. But in India, a national election takes six weeks. That is because of the large number of voters. In 2014, more than 814 million Indians could vote.

The voting machines are the size of briefcases and run on batteries. The votes are counted on the machines. Then the boxes are hauled to the next village. It might be high up in the Himalayas. The election workers might have to carry the voting machines through knee-deep snow. They will even ride elephants through lion-filled forests if that is where a voter lives.

India has 29 states and seven **territories**. They are led by a prime minister. The prime minister is the head of the government. India also has a president and vice president. They have less power than the prime minister. India's

Parliament makes the country's laws and chooses the country's prime minister.

The capital of India is New Delhi. It is known for its wide streets lined with trees on both sides. The city's main street is Rajpath. It stretches 1.5 miles (2.4 km) from a memorial called the India Gate to the president's home. Government buildings line the Rajpath.

An Indian woman casts her vote during a national election.

New Delhi is also known for the Taj Mahal. It is a white marble building. The emperor Shah Jahan built the Taj Mahal in honor of his wife after she died in 1631. Tourists from around the world come to visit the Taj Mahal. It has become a symbol of India.

Another important city in India is Mumbai. It has 19.7 million people and is India's biggest city. It is located along the Arabian Sea. India's major banks and businesses are here. It is also home to Bollywood, India's film industry.

Indian currency

Indian flag

It took more than 20,000 workers from India, Persia, Europe, and the Ottoman Empire to build the Taj Mahal.

India trades with nations around the world. Countries turn to India for food, jewelry, and other goods. Pearls are one of India's biggest exports to other countries. India is also the world's second largest exporter of cotton. Indian films, books, and music are popular worldwide.

A worker carries cotton to a factory where it will be made into fabric.

In 2014, an Indian man named Kailash Satyarthi received one of the world's highest honors. The award was the Nobel Peace Prize. Satyarthi works hard to keep Indian children in school.

FUN FACT

ONE WORLD. MANY COUNTRIES

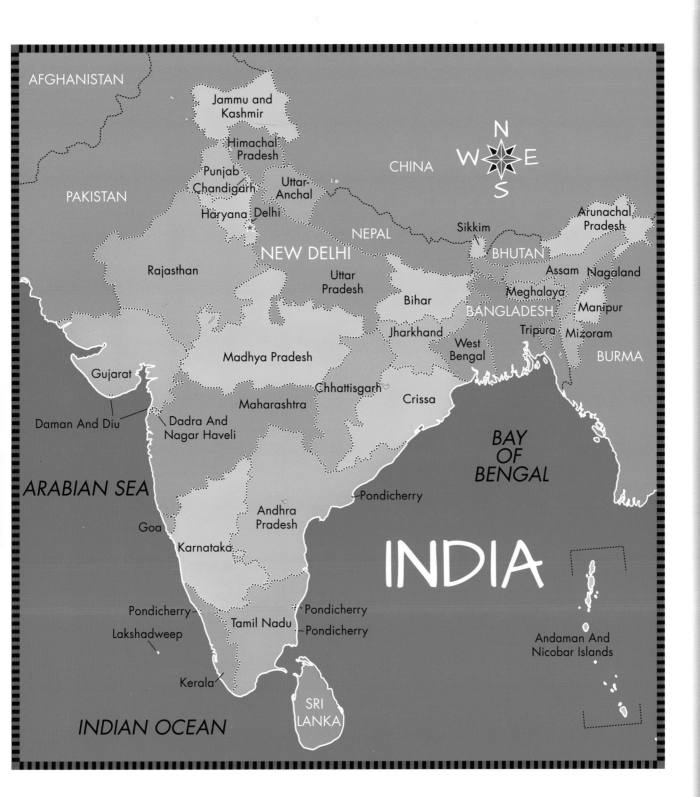

AFGHANISTAN

Jammu and Kashmir

Himachal Pradesh

CHINA

PAKISTAN

Punjab

Chandigarh

Uttar-Anchal

Haryana

Delhi

Sikkim

Arunachal Pradesh

NEW DELHI

NEPAL

BHUTAN

Assam

Nagaland

Rajasthan

Uttar Pradesh

Meghalaya

Bihar

BANGLADESH

Manipur

Jharkhand

Tripura

Mizoram

West Bengal

BURMA

Madhya Pradesh

Gujarat

Chhattisgarh

Crissa

Maharashtra

Daman And Diu

Dadra And Nagar Haveli

BAY OF BENGAL

ARABIAN SEA

Pondicherry

Goa

Andhra Pradesh

INDIA

Karnataka

Pondicherry

Pondicherry

Tamil Nadu

Pondicherry

Lakshadweep

Andaman And Nicobar Islands

Kerala

SRI LANKA

INDIAN OCEAN

GLOBAL CONNECTIONS

India's workforce is growing! Experts predict India's **economy** will be bigger than the U.S. economy by 2020. One area that is growing fast is technology. In fact, IBM (a U.S. technology company) has more workers in India than in the United States.

India has a highly trained workforce. But workers need more education. Every year, millions of young people apply to college in India. There are not enough spots for them. That means many Indians must study outside the country. Many Indian students attend universities in the United States. They might even stay in the United States to work.

Many people who leave the country to study or work later return to India. Every year, there are more jobs back home. Companies around the world team up with India to do business. In one month, leaders of both Amazon and Facebook visited India. They know that India has workers who can make their Web sites run better.

U.S. companies can also pay lower wages to workers in India than in the United States. People in the United States who call a phone number for technical support may hear an Indian voice. Those jobs help India's economy grow.

CHAPTER 4

PEOPLE AND CULTURES

More than 1.25 billion people live in India. Eight out of ten Indians are Hindu. It is one of the world's oldest religions. Hindus believe that cows are **sacred**. That is one reason why Hindus are vegetarians. They will not hurt other creatures. Hindus also believe in **karma**. If they do good things for others, they believe good things will happen to them.

Because Hindus believe cows are sacred, cows are allowed to roam the streets freely in India.

When Hindus greet someone, they look like they're praying. They bow their heads, palms together, and say, "Namaste" or "Namaskar." In the ancient language of Sanskrit, these words mean "I bow to you." Hindus try to treat everyone, especially older people, with respect.

Islam is another religion practiced in India. In 1206 AD, Muslims conquered India. The religion they practiced was Islam. Soon Islam became an important religion in India. Today, Muslims are India's second biggest religious group. Muslims pray five times a day. Their god is called Allah. Their holy book is the Koran.

More than 1,000 languages are spoken in India. But more than half of the people speak Hindi. It is the country's official language. Students are required to study it in school. English is taught in private schools and universities. Educated Indians speak English. When they speak on the phone or travel to other countries to do business, they usually speak English.

Indians also celebrate holidays. January 26 is Republic Day in India. It is a national holiday for remembering when India's constitution became law in 1950. Camels and elephants march in a parade through the capital of New Delhi.

August 15 is Independence Day. The country marks
its independence from Great Britain in 1947. Indian leader
Mahatma Gandhi helped India gain its independence. On
October 2, the nation honors Gandhi's birthday.

Religious festivals are also important in India. In the spring
people hold the Hindu festival called Holi. It celebrates the
victory of good over evil and is a festival of color. Children and

A Muslim man prays at the Jama
Masjid Mosque in Old Delhi.

adults squirt colored water at each other. They throw handfuls of pink or red powder. Kids fill balloons with colored water and throw them at their friends.

Diwali is a Hindu holiday called the Festival of Lights. Diwali means "row of lamps." Indians light lamps for Lakshmi, the goddess of wealth. Diwali is celebrated for five days and marks the beginning of the Hindu new year. Children wear new clothes, and everyone eats sweets and gives gifts. Fireworks brighten the sky.

Children are covered in powdered dyes during a celebration at a Holi festival.

Indians love and respect elephants. A Hindu god named Ganesha has the head of an elephant. Elephants march at religious festivals and weddings. At the Elephant Festival in the city of Jaipur, elephants are painted bright colors. They wear fancy rugs and ankle bells.

FUN FACT

ONE WORLD · MANY COUNTRIES

30 np

CHAPTER 5

DAILY LIFE

India has more than 440 million children.

India is a large country with a growing population. The country is filled with young people. One in three people living in India is younger than 15.

Daily life in India varies greatly. In India's cities, families live in modern homes that have indoor plumbing, phones, and computers. Children attend school and play with friends.

Women in Rajasthan, India, balance water jugs on their heads. They must collect water from wells every day because their homes have no indoor plumbing.

In rural areas daily lives are much different. Families may live in homes made of mud, straw, and tin. Their homes often do not have electricity, phones, or indoor toilets. Most rural homes are part of a larger village. The villages often have narrow streets, a public well, and fields nearby.

Traditional Indian food uses a variety of spices. It might be a curry sauce, or *saag paneer* (spinach and cheese). A popular dessert is *gulab jamun*, golden dumplings soaked in sugary syrup. Family meals are important. Many families dinner together. If families do not have a table, they sit on mats on the floor.

Saris are often made from bright fabric with designs. It can take up to 7 yards (6.4 m) of fabric to make one sari.

Women in India often wear saris. Saris are long, colorful pieces of cloth. To wear one, a woman wraps the sari around her waist several times. Then she drapes the rest of the cloth over her shoulder. Sometimes the extra cloth goes over her head, like a hood. Saris are worn over a skirt and a short shirt called a *choli*.

Some women chose to save their saris for special occasions. They wear another type of traditional clothing called the *shalwar-kamiz*. This outfit is made up of loose pants and a long shirt. The *shalwar-kamiz* is most commonly worn by women who live in large cities.

Traffic is loud and hectic in India. Cars, bikes, buses, scooters, carts, elephants, and rickshaws all travel on narrow roads. If a cow lies down in the middle of the street, everyone has to skirt around it.

FUN FACT

ONE WORLD • MANY COUNTRIES

This woman wears a traditional sari while working at a modern call center in India.

Men also have traditional clothing. One piece of clothing is called a *dhoti*. It is a long piece of white cloth that is wrapped around the legs and knotted at the waist. It is worn like a pair of pants. On top, Indian men often wear a *kurta*. It is a loose shirt that reaches down to the knees. Clothing such as business suits and blue jeans are also becoming popular, especially in large cities.

Only a few Indians own cars. There are buses and trains to take them to work. Around 7,500 trains carry 11 million people each day. The trains are very crowded. Some people climb on the roof for a seat.

From Himalayan mountain villages to big cities such as Mumbai, India is a unique country. Its population is growing, and its people are contributing to the world with their many talents.

DAILY LIFE FOR CHILDREN

Children do not need babysitters in India. They often live with their mothers, aunts, and grandmothers. Everyone helps care for them.

Mothers get up early to make breakfast. They pack their children's lunch in a *tiffin*. That is a steel lunchbox. Lunch might be flatbread, a vegetable dish, and mangoes.

School is free for children aged six to 14. After that parents have to pay for school and books. Many students wear uniforms. When school is over, they play games such as chess, soccer, or cricket. Cricket is a game that is a bit like baseball, but uses a paddle and ball.

FAST FACTS

Population: 1.2 billion

Area: 1,269,219 square miles (3,287,262 sq km)

Capital: New Delhi

Largest Cities: New Delhi, Mumbai, and Kolkata

Form of Government: Federal Republic

Languages: Hindi and English

Trading Partners:
United States, the European
Union, and China

Major Holidays:
Republic Day, Independence Day,
Gandhi's birthday

National Dish: Rice, Curry
(a spicy stew), Roti (flatbread),
and Dal (a spicy bean sauce)

School girls visit the
Sri Meenakshi Amman Temple.

GLOSSARY

democracy (di-MOCK-ruh-see) A democracy is a form of government where people vote for their leaders. India is a democracy.

economy (ih-KON-uh-me) An economy is how a country runs its industry, trade, and finance. India's economy is growing.

exports (EX-portz) Exports are food, clothing, or other goods that one country sells to other countries. Jewelry is one of India's main exports.

karma (KAR-muh) Hindus believe that karma is the result of a person's actions. It determines what a person's future may be. The idea of karma is part of daily life in India.

peninsula (puh-NIN-suh-luh) A peninsula is a piece of land that is almost completely surrounded by water. The Indian Ocean circles the southern tip of the Indian peninsula.

plateau (pla-TOH) A plateau is raised, flat land. Monkeys scamper through the forest on the plateau.

sacred (SAY-krid) Something that is sacred is holy, loved, and respected. Cows are sacred in India.

territories (TER-uh-tor-eez) Territories are large areas of land controlled by a nation, state, or ruler. India has seven territories.

To Learn More

BOOKS

Apte, Sunita. *India*. New York: Children's Press, 2009.

Bartell, Jim. *India*. Minneapolis, MN: Bellwether Media, 2011.

Gandhi, Arun. *Grandfather Gandhi*. New York: Atheneum Books for Young Readers, 2014.

WEB SITES

Visit our Web site for links about India: **childsworld.com/links**

Note to Parents, Teachers, and Librarians: We routinely verify our Web links to make sure they are safe and active sites. So encourage your readers to check them out!

Index